Under the Sun

Under the Sun

WRITTEN AND ILLUSTRATED BY

ELLEN KANDOIAN

DODD, MEAD & COMPANY

New York

1   2   3   4   5   6   7   8   9   10

Designed by Kathleen Westray

Library of Congress Cataloging-in-Publication Data

Kandoian, Ellen.
Under the sun.

Summary: Molly's mother answers her question about
where the sun goes each night by taking her on a visual
journey around the world.
1. Sun—Juvenile literature.   2. Day—Juvenile literature.   3. Night—Juvenile literature.   [1. Sun.   2. Day.
3. Night]   I. Title.
QB521.5.K36   1987   525'.3   87-5328
ISBN 0-396-09059-1

For my parents,
ARMIG and JANE

"**W**here does the sun go when I go to bed?"
Molly asked her mother.

Her mother replied, "While you are sleeping…

It goes to the Mississippi River where

a little boy watches it set from his houseboat.

Then it goes to the Great Plains where a little girl

watches it go down over the prairie.

Then on to the Rocky Mountains where an elk

sees it set high behind a mountain peak.

Then it goes to San Francisco where

the sea gulls can't see it because it's raining.

The sun goes to Hawaii where a brother and sister

watch it go down over the Pacific Ocean.

Then it goes to Japan where

a little girl watches it set from her garden.

The sun goes to China where a panda
watches it disappear among the trees.

Then it goes to the Mongolian Desert where a camel

watches it set behind the dunes.

Then the sun goes to a town in eastern Russia
where there is a little boy who is going to bed.

And maybe he is wondering,
'Where does the sun go when I go to bed?'

Just then, while he is wondering—

and the camel,

and the panda,

and the Japanese girl,

and the Hawaiian children,

and the sea gulls,

and the elk,

and the girl on the prairie,

and the boy in the houseboat are sleeping,

The sun will come in your window
and wake you up!"

HOW DOES IT HAPPEN?

Through science, people have learned about the sun and the Earth. Our world—the Earth—is round like a ball. The sun is a big light far away in space. The Earth slowly turns each day, but the sun stays still.

While half of the Earth is in sunlight, the other half is in darkness. So while Molly is going to bed at eight o'clock on the East Coast of the United States as it is getting dark, half a world away in eastern Russia it is getting light. By the time she wakes up, it is time for the little boy in eastern Russia to go to bed.

If you want to see how the sun shines on the Earth, do this experiment. You need a big ball, a flashlight, and a friend to help you. If you have a globe, use that as your big ball.

In a dark room, have your friend turn on the flashlight. Hold the ball directly in the light of the flashlight, so that half of the ball is in the light. The flashlight is like the sun. The big ball is like the Earth. The bright side is having daylight, while the dark side is having night.

Turn the ball (Earth) slowly, keeping the top and bottom still. Look at one spot on the ball (Earth) and see how it goes from light (day) to dark (night). Each day, as the Earth turns away from the sun, we enter the dark side once at sunset, and we enter the bright side once at sunrise.